Cuando Sea Grande / When I Grow Up

PUEDO SER UNA BAILARINA/ I CAN BE A BALLERINA

By Alex Appleby   Traducido por Eida de la Vega

Gareth Stevens
PUBLISHING

Please visit our website, www.garethstevens.com. For a free color catalog of all our high-quality books, call toll free 1-800-542-2595 or fax 1-877-542-2596.

Library of Congress Cataloging-in-Publication Data

Appleby, Alex.
I can be a ballerina = Puedo ser una bailarina / by Alex Appleby, translated by Eida de la Vega.
p. cm. — (When I grow up = Cuando sea grande)
Parallel title: Cuando sea grande
In English and Spanish.
Includes index.
ISBN 978-1-4824-0857-7 (library binding)
1. Ballerinas — Juvenile literature. I. Appleby, Alex. II. Title.
GV1787.5 A66 2015
792.8—d23

First Edition

Published in 2015 by
Gareth Stevens Publishing
111 East 14th Street, Suite 349
New York, NY 10003

Copyright © 2015 Gareth Stevens Publishing

Editor: Ryan Nagelhout
Designer: Sarah Liddell
Spanish Translation: Eida de la Vega

Photo credits: Cover, p. 1 (dancer) iStock/Thinkstock.com; cover, p. 1 (main) Karramba Production/Shutterstock.com; p. 5 AntonioDiaz/Shutterstock.com; p. 7 CREATISTA/Shutterstock.com; p. 9 Zero CreativesCultura/Getty Images; pp. 11, 13 Fuse/Fuse/Thinkstock.com; p. 15 LiAndStudio/Shutterstock.com; p. 17 Digital Vision/Photodisc/Thinkstock.com; p. 19 Sean Nel/Shuttertstock.com; p. 21 Fuse/Fuse/Thinkstock.com; pp. 23, 24 (slippers) Michael Guttman/iStock/Thinkstock.com.

Printed in the United States of America

CPSIA compliance information: Batch #CS15GS: For further information contact Gareth Stevens, New York, New York at 1-800-542-2595.

Contenido

- -

Contents

Me encanta bailar.

I love to dance.

Es divertido
hacer ejercicio.

It is fun to exercise.

Tomo muchas
clases de baile.

I take many
dance classes.

Mi maestra es
una bailarina.

My teacher is
a ballerina.

¡Cuando sea grande
yo también quiero
ser bailarina!

I want to be one
when I grow up, too!

13

Tengo mucho
que aprender.

There is a lot to learn.

Aprendo los pasos.
Se llaman posiciones.

- -

I learn the steps.
These are
called positions.

Hay cinco posiciones.

- -

There are
five positions.

Uso zapatos especiales.
Son zapatillas de ballet.

I wear special shoes.
These are slippers.

¡Mis zapatillas
son rosadas!

My slippers are pink!

23

Palabras que debes saber/ Words to Know

(las) zapatillas/ slippers

Índice/Index